ELEMENTARY HARMONY

HARMONY

PART II

BY

C. H. KITSON

M.A. Cantab., D.Mus. Oxon.

SOMETIME PROFESSOR OF MUSIC, UNIVERSITY COLLEGE, DUBLIN
SENIOR PROFESSOR OF THEORY, ROYAL IRISH
ACADEMY OF MUSIC, DUBLIN

LONDON
OXFORD UNIVERSITY PRESS
NEW YORK   TORONTO

Oxford University Press, Ely House, London W. 1

GLASGOW NEW YORK TORONTO MELBOURNE WELLINGTON
CAPE TOWN SALISBURY IBADAN NAIROBI LUSAKA ADDIS ABABA
BOMBAY CALCUTTA MADRAS KARACHI LAHORE DACCA
KUALA LUMPUR HONG KONG

FIRST PUBLISHED 1920
REPRINTED 1921, 1926, 1929, 1933
1937, 1940, 1945, 1947, 1949, 1951
1956, 1961, 1963, 1966

PRINTED IN GREAT BRITAIN
AT THE UNIVERSITY PRESS, OXFORD
BY VIVIAN RIDLER
PRINTER TO THE UNIVERSITY

PREFACE

THIS part concludes diatonic harmony. It has been necessary to discuss some chromatic harmony, but only a very limited amount—e.g. that involved by the use of dominant fundamental harmony of the minor key in the major key, and by the employment of transition as opposed to gradual modulation. Part III will deal with chromatic harmony in general.

It is hoped that the use of various types of exercises will give the student the power to use the resource discussed in some practical fashion, and also give the mind the training that the figured bass denies. The Exercises have been made simple and short, as the students for whom this book is intended have not much time to devote to the subject. But it has been my aim to enable them to spend what little time they have to the best advantage.

C. H. KITSON.

CONTENTS

CHAPTER I

DIATONIC CHORDS OF THE SEVENTH

1. If a diatonic seventh from the root be added to the diatonic triads of the key (except V), the resultant chords are
termed diatonic sevenths.

Ex. 1.
C major.

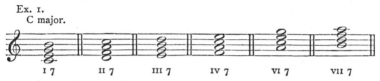

I 7   II 7   III 7   IV 7   VI 7   VII 7

2. In employing these chords:

(*a*) The discord of the seventh must be 'prepared' by
occurring in the same part in the previous chord;

(*b*) The discord must resolve one step downwards into a
chord of which such resolution is the third.

It will be obvious that IV 7 and VII 7 will be rarely used, as
IV will resolve into VII and VII into III. They are common
in the course of a sequence, e.g. a passage framed on at least
two chords, repeated at a different pitch (see ×).

Ex. 2.

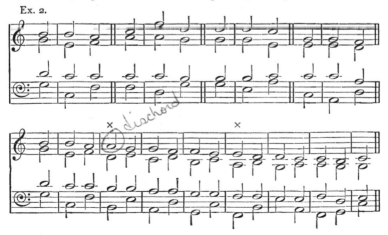

3. If the third in one chord remains to be the seventh in the next, a chain of sevenths may be produced.

Ex. 3.

(*a*) The doubling of the leading note, as the result of the repetition of a pattern forming a sequence, is allowable.

4. First inversions need no extra explanation.

Ex. 4.

5. Second inversions are rare, because of the difficulty of satisfactory approach. Generally some other harmony is preferable.

Ex. 5.

The beginner is recommended to leave them alone. The bass of any second inversion is under the same restrictions as the bass of an ordinary six-four as regards the manner of approaching and quitting it.

6. Third inversions:

7. Inversions resolving into other chords of the seventh:

8. II 7 gives a new approach to the Perfect, False, or Imperfect Cadence.

9. The Minor Key.

Secondary sevenths involving the leading note are practically useless. Those involving the flattened leading note should not be attempted in elementary work. II 7 and VI 7 are the only diatonic sevenths that will be considered in this chapter.

Ex. 9.

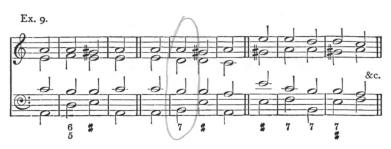

10. As the cadential six-four is a decoration of the five-three into which it resolves, II 7 can proceed to this before finally resolving, the seventh remaining to be the fourth from the bass note in the six-four.   II 7 of the minor key is also available in the major key.

Ex. 10.

Ear-tests.

Ex. 11.

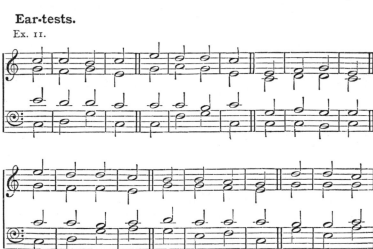

(*a*) Ornamental resolution.

Exercises.

(1) Add parts for A. and T., introducing some unessential notes :

(2) Add parts for A. T.:

(3) Harmonize the following Cadences, using the diatonic chord of the seventh on the supertonic in approaching them:

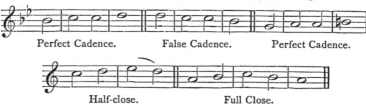

Perfect Cadence.   False Cadence.   Perfect Cadence.

Half-close.   Full Close.

(4) Continue the following sequences for a few bars, and end in an appropriate manner:

(5) Figure the following basses and add parts for S. A. T., introducing secondary sevenths and unessential notes:

(6) Precede and follow the given chords by other chords in the keys stated :

G major.

(a)   (b)   (c)   (d)

E minor.

(a)   (b)

(7) Harmonize the following for S. A. T. B., introducing diatonic chords of the seventh :

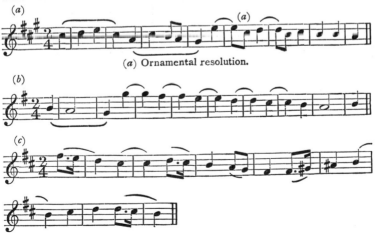

(a) Ornamental resolution.

(8) Continue the following sequences for a few bars, and conclude:

CHAPTER II

PARTICULAR USES OF SOME
DIATONIC SEVENTHS

1. II 7 in the first inversion can be used as if the sixth from the bass were added to IV*a*; for this reason it is called the chord of the added sixth. It can resolve on to I*a*.

Ex. 12.

C major.　　　　　A minor.

The same procedure may be used with VI 7 in the first inversion.

Ex. 13.

In the minor key the sixth degree of the scale will be sharpened.

2. Provided that a discord resolve one step downwards, there is no fixed rule as to what chord shall form the resolution. Therefore:

(*a*) IV 7 may resolve into V, or V decorated by the six-four on its bass note.

Ex. 14.

Also in minor key.

In the first inversion the seventh should be sounded *above* the root, else the effect is unpleasant.   Other inversions are not recommended.

(*b*) VI 7 may resolve into a dominant seventh.

Ex. 15.

In the minor key the sixth degree of the scale is sharpened.

Ex. 16.

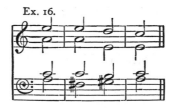

(c) VII 7 may resolve into a dominant seventh, or into the tonic chord.

Ex. 17.

In the major key, when resolving into the tonic chord, this is called the Chord of the Leading Seventh. In the minor key it is termed the Chord of the Diminished Seventh.

In the inversions, in the major key the seventh should be sounded above the root.

Ex. 18.

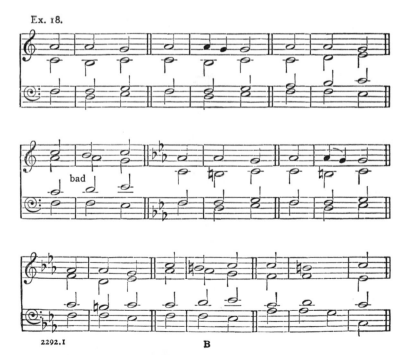

No two parts may proceed from 7 to 8.

Ex. 19.

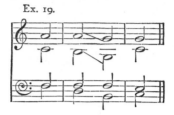

Observe that in all these cases a correct bass will move by step or remain stationary in quitting the chord of the seventh.

3. In all these particular uses, the seventh of the root *may* be taken without preparation.

Ex. 20.

4. The diminished seventh of the minor key may be used in the tonic major key.

Ex. 21.

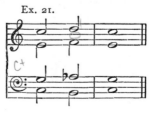

It is in this case a chromatic discord : that is to say, it contains a sound not found in the diatonic scale of the key. Designate the chord thus: VII$_{b7}$, or VII$_{\natural 7}$, as the case may be.

Ear-tests.

All the examples of this chapter, except those illustrating faults, may be employed as ear-tests.

Exercises.

Ex. 22.

(1) Harmonize the following cadences, using the chord of the added sixth:

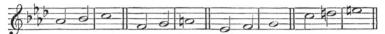

(2) Write chords to precede and follow the given chords in as many ways as you deem appropriate:

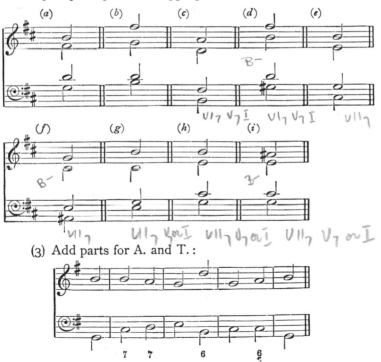

(3) Add parts for A. and T.:

(4) Harmonize the following in four parts, illustrating the particular uses of diatonic sevenths discussed:

(5) Figure and harmonize the following basses:

CHAPTER III

CHANGING NOTES, ANTICIPATIONS, AND CHROMATIC PASSING NOTES

1. Two statements of the same harmony note may be separated by the use of the unessential notes a step above and below
such harmony in either order.

Ex. 23.

But, when such harmony note is the root of the chord, the
lower unessential note must be a semitone below it, unless the
next harmony note be a third below the original one.

Ex. 23 a.

When such harmony note is the fifth of the chord, the lower
unessential note must be a semitone below it, unless the second
displaces the third as the fourth displaces the fifth.

Ex. 23 *b.*

ugly   good   good

2. Two harmony notes a third apart (the second being lower than the first) may be separated by the unessential note a step below the first, followed by that a step below the second.

Ex. 24.
(*a*)   (*b*)   (*c*)   (*d*)

The unessential note below the root must be a semitone from it, unless it falls a third to the succeeding harmony note (see (*c*) and (*d*)). In the following example the idiom is retained, but the third quaver is the harmony note. The fourth quaver should rise one step, according to ancient convention.

Ex. 25.

3. Two harmony notes a third apart (the second being higher than the first) may be separated by the unessential note a step above the first, followed by that a step above the second.

Ex. 26.

All these are examples of changing notes.

4. The two harmony notes connected by the changing notes may be factors of different chords.

Ex. 26 *a*.

5. When two harmony notes are a step apart, the second being lower than the first, the unessential note next above the first may leap down a third to the second.

Ex. 27.

Ex. 28.

6. Somewhat rarely the reverse procedure is employed.

Ex. 29.

7. These idioms must not be confused with the use of appoggiaturas.

Ex. 30.

8. The idiom explained in paragraph 1 may be curtailed by the omission of the initial note.

Ex. 31.

9. When two harmony notes are a step apart, the second may be anticipated over the harmony of the first. The note employing this device is termed an anticipation. It is generally used in the top part, or in the top part combined with another. Do not strike other harmony notes with the anticipation.

Ex. 32.

10. Passing and auxiliary notes used between statements of the same chord may be anticipated.

Ex. 33.

11. Chromatic passing notes may be employed. Care must be taken that the chromatic semitone below the major third of the chord (used either as a passing note, appoggiatura, or auxiliary note) has not the effect of being the minor third.

Ex. 34.

It is generally agreed that, in order to ensure uniformity of style, once a chromatic passing note is introduced, the part must proceed in semitones till a harmony note is reached.

Ex. 35.

12. It is not good to alter a passing note chromatically to become a harmony note.

Ex. 36.

In the above example F cannot be regarded as being E sharp. We cannot chromatically raise the major third of a chord.

Ex. 37.

13. The collision of the major and minor thirds over dominant harmony in the minor key is allowed, thus:

Ex. 38.

Take care in such a case that the minor third is of quite short duration.

14. Ear-tests may be selected from the examples in this chapter.

Exercises.

(1) Re-write the soprano parts in the following, introducing the unessential resource indicated :

Ex. 39.

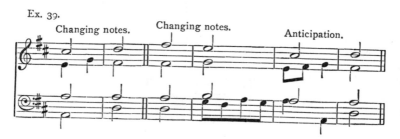

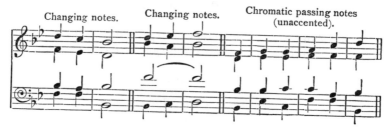

(2) Harmonize the following fragments in four parts :

(3) Add inner parts to the following:

(4) Add S. A. T. in accordance with the figures:

8 - 7 -   3 2 4 3   8 - 7 -   5 6 5
3 4 2 3   5 ♮4 6 5   3 4 3
                               3 ——

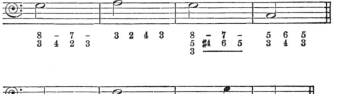

10 9 7 8   8 7 9 8   8 ♯7 6 5

3 - 2 8 - 7   6   4 3   6   5 - 4
      ♯6 ——   4   ♮ ——

(5) Harmonize the following for S. A. T. B.:

CHAPTER IV

ELEMENTARY MODULATION. (*a*)

1. MODULATION is 'the process of passing out of one key into another' (GROVE).

A new key is established when the dominant of this key is followed by its tonic, provided that either contains a note foreign to the key quitted.

The following is not a modulation from C major to F major, because all the chords are diatonic in C major:

Ex. 40.

2. The process of modulation is carried out by approaching a chord as belonging to the first key and quitting it as belonging to the new key, and then adding the Perfect Cadence. A modulation from C major to F major would be produced (*a*) by adding the minor seventh to the dominant of F, or (*b*) by preceding this dominant chord by a chord belonging to F major but not to C major.

Ex. 41.
(*a*)   (*b*)

{ II C major.
{ VI F major.

{ II C major.
{ VI F major.

3. Although a key is only actually confirmed by dominant to tonic, yet it must be conceded that this direct confirmation is not always necessary or desirable. A False Close does not take away the effect of a new key, it merely avoids finality in it. The same may be said of the Half-close.

Ex. 42.

(a)   (b)

These procedures will give variety in cadences.

4. Generally speaking, the process of modulation is satisfactory if completed in at least four chords:

(a) The tonic chord of the first key.

(b) The pivot chord with the dual relation, being neither the tonic of the first key nor the tonic or the dominant of the second key.

(c) The dominant of the new key.

(d) The tonic of the new key.

Ex. 43.

{ VI C major.
{ II G major.

5. This chapter will be concerned with modulation to nearly related keys, e.g. tonic, dominant, and subdominant with their relatives:

		A minor.	E minor.	D minor.
C major.	Related keys.		G major.	F major.
A minor.	Related keys.	C major.	E minor.	D minor
			G major.	F major.

6. It is not always possible with the present resource to avoid the tonic of either key as the pivot chord :

(*a*) Modulation from C major to D minor.

D minor is the only diatonic chord with a dual relation.

(*b*) A minor to E minor.

A minor must be the pivot chord.

(*c*) A minor to G major.

A minor must be the pivot chord.

(*d*) A minor to D minor.

D minor must be the pivot chord.

Thus the process of modulation can be carried out in three chords, or in more than four.

Ex. 44.

C major to G major.

{ vi. C major.
{ ii. G major.

{ i C major.
{ iv G major.

{ vi C major.
{ ii G major.

C major to A minor.   C major to E minor.   C major to F major.

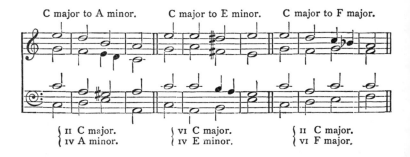

{ ii C major.
{ iv A minor.

{ vi C major.
{ iv E minor.

{ ii C major.
{ vi F major.

7. In modulating from a minor key to its subdominant minor (A minor to D minor) it is better to introduce at least one chord belonging to the new key after the pivot chord, to avoid the unpleasant juxtaposition of the major and minor forms of the same chord (A minor and A major).

Be careful to avoid such an ugly part as:

Ex. 45.

Put C natural and C sharp in different parts.

8. A modulation is usually confirmed at a cadence.

In harmonizing a melody, note that the melody may either express the modulation by having the necessary accidental, or imply it by its formation.

Ex. 46.

9. Sometimes the actual modulation is made in the course of a phrase and then confirmed with a Full Close at the end. In such a case avoid the new tonic in *root* position in the middle of the phrase on the strong accent.

In (*a*), I occurs in the root position on the weak accent.

In (*b*), I occurs in the first inversion on the strong accent.

In (*b*), V could have been followed by VI instead of I*b*.

10. If two modulations occur in a phrase, one during its course, and the other at the end, the former should have its I in the first inversion, or use V to VI.

Ex. 48.

11. When there is no chord common to the two keys, the modulation is termed abrupt; the procedure is also called a transition. In this case the connecting link is a note in common. This procedure is useful in the middle of phrases, except the first, or in sub-phrases. It should not be used at the end of normal phrases.

Ex. 49.

C major to A minor.   C major to D minor.

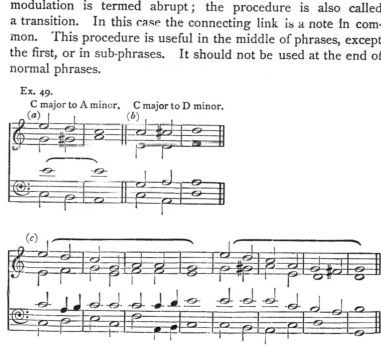

(*a*) and (*b*) are examples of transitions.

(*c*) gives two phrases, in the second there is a transition followed by a modulation.

(*d*) is an example of the bad use of transition.

12. Transitions provide opportunities for the use of sequence, the progression V to I being used in two or more keys.

When the qualities of the intervals forming the chords in each statement are the same, the sequence is real. This can occur when the two keys are both major or minor.

Ex. 50.

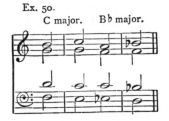

But when one key is major and another minor, or vice versa, the qualities of the intervals forming the chords cannot be exactly reproduced. The sequence is then free.

Diatonic sequences must be free.

Modulating sequences are either strict (real) or free.

Ex. 51.

13. A section of melody such as follows often causes students trouble:

Ex. 52.
End of phrase.

(a)   (b)

(*a*) is obviously a modulation to G major. At (*b*), the only satisfactory treatment of B flat is to regard it as the seventh of the root C. Thus, if the major third of a chord be immediately chromatically flattened, treat the flattened note as a discord.

Ex. 53.

&c.

14. When the major or minor third of a chord is chromatically altered to become the minor or major third of the same chord, or the root or fifth of another chord (following it in consecutive order), such altered note must be kept in the same part, other-wise the unpleasant effect termed False Relation is produced.

Ex. 54.

Bearing in mind the facts that (*a*) false relation is caused by placing in unpleasant juxtaposition chords that produce confusion of tonality, (*b*) the addition of the minor seventh to a major common chord does not alter its derivation, it will be obvious that the question of false relation does not enter into such a case as the following:

Ex. 55.

There is no false relation between the chords of G and C.

15. False relation is said to occur with a chord intervening as in the following case:

Ex. 56.

But the false relation is considered unobjectionable—

(*a*) in the Tierce de Picardie;

(*b*) in using the minor seventh of the minor scale as a harmony note.

Ex. 57.

16. Ex. 44 should be used for ear-tests.

17. The exercises in this chapter will be concerned only with the processes of modulation and transition. Their application in framing sentences will be considered in the next chapter.

Exercises.

✓ (1) Imitating the procedures in Ex. 44, modulate in a few chords from:—(a) F major to C major, (b) G major to E minor, (c) D major to F sharp minor, (d) D major to G major, (e) G major to A minor, (f) E minor to G major, (g) E minor to B minor, (h) B minor to A major, (i) B minor to E minor, (j) E minor to C major.

✓ (2) Write transitions from (a) D major to E minor, (b) F major to D minor.

✓ (3) Harmonize the following, introducing the modulations expressed or implied (the sections end with Full Closes in the new key; all begin in B flat major):

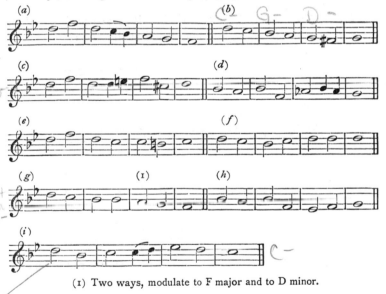

(1) Two ways, modulate to F major and to D minor.

(4) Harmonize the following, introducing the modulations expressed or implied (the sections end with Full Closes in the new key; all begin in F minor):

(5) Add parts for S. A. T. Modulations are anticipated in the course of the phrases, and confirmed at the end:

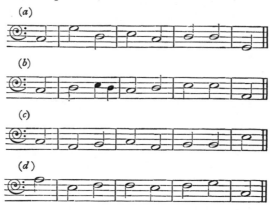

(6) Harmonize the following, introducing both transition and modulation in the same section:

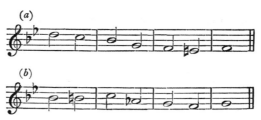

(7) Harmonize the following sections as modulating sequences:

(a)

G minor.　　　　F major.

(b)

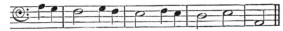

B♭ major.　　　　G minor.

(8) Harmonize the following sections of bass:

(a) Diatonic sequence:

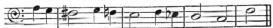

(b) Modulating sequence (free):

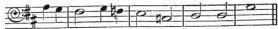

(c) Modulating sequence (strict):

(d) Modulating sequence (free):

CHAPTER V

ELEMENTARY MODULATION. (*b*)

1. THIS chapter deals with the application of modulation in forming sentences or periods, or in harmonizing melodies or basses producing them.

A sentence in music consists of two phrases, each normally four bars long. This, however, is too short for any extended scheme of modulation.

If another sentence be added, sixteen bars in all, a cycle of modulations will be satisfactory in effect.

2. This period of sixteen bars is generally considered as divisible into two equal parts (Binary form). In deciding upon a scheme of modulation for the whole, the following points must be carefully borne in mind :

(*a*) The tonic key should be thoroughly established before modulation takes place. Therefore it is advisable not to modulate in the first phrase at all : a Full Close in the tonic at the end of the first phrase is quite possible.

(*b*) The second phrase should end with a Full Close in some key *not* on the flat side of the tonic. This modulation must be gradual, and it may be preceded by some other transition or modulation with its tonic in the first inversion, or any other appropriate means of avoiding finality.

(*c*) More frequent modulation may occur in the second half. Often the third phrase splits up into two smaller sections utilizing sequence. This is the place for modulation on to the flat side. Avoid new tonics in root position on the strong accents.

(*d*) The fourth phrase may have modulation at its outset, but time must be given to re-establish the tonic by gradual modulation.

Thus the following is a good scheme:

Bars 1–4, C major.
,, 5–8, through A minor to G major.
,, 9–12, F major, D minor.
,, 13–16, back to C.

Ex. 58.

3. In the above example all the modulations are confirmed by the use of V to I. This could be avoided sometimes, but not

always. At (*a*) a Half-close could have been used, but the dominant would have to be followed by the tonic, for the use of V to
VI would demand the chord of F major, which would make the
modulation to G major abrupt.

Ex. 59.

There could have been either a False Close or Half-close at
(*b*). A False Close at (*c*) would be poor, as the chord of B flat
puts the mind off C major, which has to be re-established.

4. A diatonic passing note in the new key which is foreign to
the key quitted, cannot be introduced until the new key has been
established, in which case it will usually have been heard as an
essential note.

Ex. 60.
(*a*)

(*b*)

5. The following points must be carefully borne in mind in harmonizing melodies or unfigured basses:

(*a*) If a given part commences with chromaticisms, every effort must be made to avoid modulation:

Ex. 61.

(*b*) On the other hand, the end of the second phrase may have no chromaticism and yet demand modulation.

Ex. 62.

(*c*) If a melody begin with a phrase or section repeated, harmonize it first without modulation, and then with it.

Ex. 63.

(*d*) If a melody seems to allure one into a Full Close in the tonic in the middle of the problem, modulation or transition is generally possible.

Ex. 64.

6. Exercises.

(1) Harmonize the following with appropriate modulations (S. A. T. B.):

None of the chromaticisms need imply modulation.

Chromatic notes imply modulation.

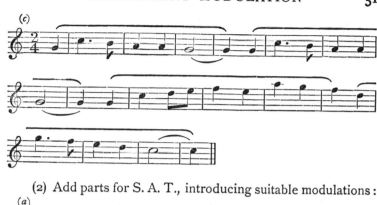

(2) Add parts for S. A. T., introducing suitable modulations:

(3) Following the plan of formation in the preceding exercises,

(*a*) Start as follows:

and proceed thus: bars 5–8, through B minor to F sharp minor; 9–10, E minor; 11–12, G major; 13–16, back to D major.

(*b*) Start as follows:

and proceed thus: bars 5–8, through C major to E minor; 9–10, F major; 11–12, B flat major; 13–16, back to A minor.

CHAPTER VI

SUSPENSIONS

1. When a part that normally proceeds by one step downwards from an essential note in one chord to an essential note in another, retards its movement until the other factors of the second chord have been struck, the retarded note at this point is called a Suspension. Its occurrence in the same part in the previous chord is termed its preparation, and its final descent into the harmony of the second chord is termed its resolution.

Ex. 65.

2. In the example (a) and in the further examples at the same

places, (1) is the preparation of the suspended discord, (2) is the suspension itself, (3) is its resolution.

3. In the examples (a), (b), and (c) the root of the chord is suspended, and the root position and two inversions are given. 9 8 implies $\frac{9\ 8}{5\ -}$; 7 6 implies $\frac{7\ 6}{3\ -}$.

4. In the examples (d), (e), (f) the third of the chord is suspended.   4 3 implies $\frac{4\ 3}{5\ -}$.

5. In (g), (h), and (i) the fifth of the chord is suspended.   6 5 implies $\frac{6\ 5}{3\ -}$.

6. The discord should not be sounded against its resolution, except the resolution be in the bass only, as at (a), (e), and (i).

Exceptionally the discord may be sounded against its resolution in an upper part by contrary and conjunct movement, but only as a last resource.   Such a procedure is excessively harsh if the suspension resolve into the third of the chord.

Ex. 66.

In the above examples (c) is better than (a), as the scalic movement of the tenor in short notes justifies the exceptional treatment.

7. The discord must be more strongly accented than its resolution.

Ex. 67.

8. Suspensions do not remove consecutives.

Ex. 68.

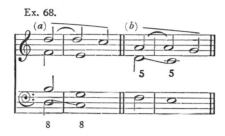

Fifths between upper parts, as in example (*b*), are not bad in effect, but the beginner is advised to use them sparingly.

9. **Suspensions in the bass.** When these are used, no upper part should sound the resolution against the discord.

Ex. 69.

(*d*) is poor, because (1) is not in effect a suspension at all, but the chord of A minor. $\frac{5}{2}$‍ and $\frac{4}{2}$‍ are the only satisfactory suspensions in the bass, and the former is much the better of the two.

10. The suspended discord may resolve on to another chord, or another position of the same chord.

Ex. 70.

11. Sometimes upward resolving suspensions are used. Only the following are recommended for elementary work:

Ex. 71.

(1) Only use when the seventh is major. The first inversion may be used, as at (d).

(b) should be used rarely. Upward resolving suspensions will be avoided in the bass for the present. (c) may be regarded as two concords. (d), however, is really the first inversion of 7 8 in the minor key.

12. Suspensions may resolve ornamentally,

(a) by leaping to, or taking by step, another factor of the chord of resolution;

(b) by taking the auxiliary note a step below the resolution;

(c) by filling in leaps of thirds in these, with a note producing conjunct movement.

Ex. 72.

✓13. Double suspensions may be used, moving in thirds or sixths:

Ex. 73.

Triple suspensions move in six-threes:

Ex. 74.

14. Sometimes a complete chord is suspended. But for the satisfactory employment of this no notes should *leap* to the factors of the chord of resolution.

Ex. 75.

good

15. The combination $\frac{7\ 6}{5\ 6}$ is very useful and satisfactory in effect, whether the 5 be prepared or not.

Ex. 76.

$$\begin{matrix} 7 & 6 & 7 & 6 \\ 5 & 6 & 5 & 6 \end{matrix}$$

16. In using $\frac{9\,8}{7\,8}$, do not sound 3 against them, as 9 and 7 so strongly indicate a separate chord.

In the first inversion this is not so.   (See Ex. 76.)

17. In using dominant harmony, the seventh may be used in conjunction with suspensions.   Memorize the following:

These combinations are catalogued by some theorists as being separate chords (dominant ninth, eleventh, and thirteenth). Used in the above way, it is much simpler to regard the sounds in question as suspensions. Unprepared, they are appoggiaturas. In using 6 5 with 7, sound 6 5 above 7.

18. Ties may be omitted at discretion.

19. In harmonizing a given part, bear in mind that the normal harmony moves uniformly. Therefore the more irregular the rhythm of a given part, the more necessary it is to find a means of maintaining regularity in harmonic rhythm.

Ex. 79.

Further, a repeated or tied note weak to strong, if descending subsequently by step, should as a rule be regarded as a suspended discord, especially if a bass.

Ex. 80.

20. Suspensions are useful as a means of avoiding bald harmony, and of keeping up movement, specially in intermediate cadences.

Ex. 81.

Exercises.

(1) Prepare and resolve the following suspensions downwards (*4 parts*):

(2) Prepare and resolve the following suspensions upwards:

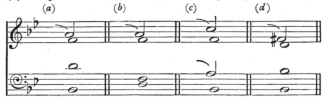

(3) Prepare and resolve the following suspensions on different positions of the same chord, or on different chords:

(4) Ornamentally resolve the following suspensions in various ways:

(5) Prepare and resolve the following double and triple suspensions:

(6) Resolve the following (*a*) as suspensions, (*b*) as appoggiaturas, in each case using a chord to precede the combination:

(7) Add parts for A. and T. to the following cadences:

(g)

√(8) Add to the following basses parts for S. A. T.:

(a)

(b)

(9) Harmonize the following for S. A. T. B. :

(a)

(b)

(c)

(10) Add parts for A. and T., introducing some suspensions in these parts; figure the result:

(11) Add parts for S. A. T. in accordance with the figures:

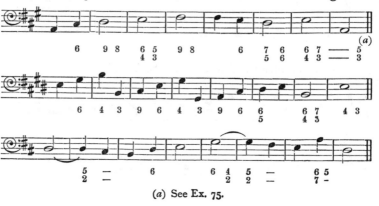

(a) See Ex. 75.

CHAPTER VII

THE CHORD OF THE DOMINANT NINTH

1. IF the diatonic ninth from the root be added to the chord of the dominant seventh, the resultant combination is called the chord of the dominant ninth.

Ex. 82.

In the chord of the dominant seventh, the seventh displaces the root and resolves upon another chord.

Ex. 83.

But the ninth can displace the root or third; and if it displace the root it can resolve while the chord remains, or upon another harmony. When the ninth resolves while the dominant harmony remains, it is merely an appoggiatura, or suspension.

Ex. 84.

When the ninth is resolving on to the root, the root should only be sounded against the discord if in the bass.

When resolving on to the third, this factor (the third) should not be sounded against the ninth.

These cases do not require further consideration here, as they are not examples of true chords of the ninth. They are merely embellishments of dominant sevenths. The minor ninth may be thus used in the major key. The major ninth may only be used in the minor key, as at (a).

2. When the ninth resolves downwards one step on to a different chord, we get a true chord of the ninth.

Ex. 85.

Here the ninth displaces the root, but resolves on to it with a different harmony.

The major ninth must be sounded above the third. The

minor ninth is used in both major and minor keys, being
chromatic in the former.   The fifth of the chord is omitted in
four parts.

Ex. 86.

3. The dominant ninth may also resolve into a secondary
seventh on the sixth degree of the scale (raised in the minor
key), if the secondary seventh resolve into a dominant seventh.

Ex. 87.

4. Inversions of the true dominant ninth (e.g. with the root
present, and the ninth resolving on to a new chord) are so rare
as to be negligible in elementary work.

When the root is absent, the chords are those of the leading
seventh and diminished seventh (see Chapter II).

5. The approach of the interval of the ninth by similar motion
between extreme parts is poor if when resolving downwards the

substitution of the resolution produces bad exposed octaves, or
actual consecutives.

6. No two parts should proceed in similar motion from 7 to 8
or from 9 to 8.

7. The chord of the diminished seventh is derived from the
dominant, and is often classified as a dominant minor ninth with
the root omitted. It consists of the major third, perfect fifth,
minor seventh, and minor ninth from the dominant root. By
altering the names of one or more of the sounds forming it,
inversions of diminished sevenths in other keys are produced.

Thus, starting with

B being the third of the root or fundamental, we can make B
the fifth of E, the seventh of C sharp, or the ninth (C♭) of B♭.

Ex. 91.

Roots G   E   C♯   B♭

(1) is the 1st inver. of dominant minor ninth in C or C minor.

(2) ,, 2nd   ,,   ,,   ,,   ,,   A or A minor.

(3) ,, 3rd   ,,   ,,   ,,   ,,   F♯ or F♯ minor.

(4) ,, 4th   ,,   ,,   ,,   ,,   E♭ or E♭ minor.

Such changes in notation are called Enharmonic.

This chord can thus be approached as being the dominant diminished seventh of one tonic, and be quitted as that of another producing modulation. The notation of the key approached should be used.

Ex. 92.

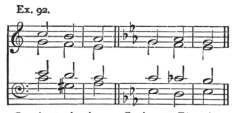

C major to A minor.   C minor to E♭ major.

Modulation to remote keys by this means is not smooth in effect.

8. In referring to dominant ninths the following abbreviations will serve:

(*a*) dominant major ninth, V_7^9.

(*b*) ,, minor ,, $V_7^{♭9}$.

9. Examples 84, 86, and 87 should be used as ear-tests.

10. **Exercises.**

(1) Precede and follow the given chords by other appropriate harmonies, treating the given chords as (*a*) dominant seventh with suspended root, (*b*) dominant seventh with appoggiatura of the root, (*c*) real dominant ninths, resolving directly into new harmony.

(2) Add parts for A. and T.; figure the result:

(3) Harmonize the following, using:

(a) Suspended ninths, (b) appoggiatura ninths, (c) ninths resolving on to different harmony as indicated (a), (b), (c).

(4) Add parts for S. A. T., introducing examples of ninths at the points indicated:

(5) Resolve the following chord in F major:

Making the necessary changes in notation, resolve it in (a) D minor, (b) B minor.

CHAPTER VIII

THE DOMINANT THIRTEENTH

1. THERE is nothing that need be catalogued as a chord of the dominant eleventh. For in using the fourth (eleventh as a compound interval) from the root over a dominant seventh, the fourth must resolve a step upwards or downwards while the rest of the chord remains. It is therefore either a suspension or an appoggiatura:

Ex. 93.   (a)

(a) It would be extremely harsh to sound B against C at (a): hence two appoggiaturas are used. Compare:

Ex. 94.

good

The fourth of the dominant chord may of course decorate the chord of the ninth as well as the seventh, or the plain common chord.

Ex. 95.

2. Just as the eleventh is a temporary displacement of the third, so the thirteenth displaces the fifth.   It must not be sounded below the seventh because of the ugly effect.

Ex. 96.

At (*a*) the thirteenth decorates the dominant common chord.
At (*b*) ,,   ,,   ,,   ,,   ,,   seventh.
At (*c*) and (*d*) the first and last inversions of the dominant seventh are thus decorated.   The second inversion is rare.

Ex. 97.

This is really VII *b*.

As the chords of the leading and diminished seventh are derivatives of the dominant, it will be convenient to catalogue here a similar decoration of them.

Ex. 98.

The minor thirteenth can be thus used only in the minor key, and the major thirteenth only in the major key.

3. But the thirteenth becomes a true factor of the chord when the above resolution is omitted, though mentally understood. In this case the thirteenth leaps down direct to the root of the tonic chord, or any chord of which this note is a factor (cf. Pt. I, p. 99).

Ex. 99.

By this principle of elision of resolution this discord may be added to the chords of the leading and diminished seventh (displacing the third from the leading note).

Ex. 100.

4. Sometimes the thirteenth remains to be a part of the next chord :

Ex. 101.

This is intelligible when it is remembered that it is merely a condensation of

Ex. 102.

5. A chromatic raising of the fifth of the chord is usually catalogued as a thirteenth, being regarded as false notation for the flattened sixth (cf. Pt. I, p. 96).

Ex. 103.

This view obtains some support from the fact that in the minor key the raised fifth would not be written, as it has to remain stationary as the third of the tonic, or else it must fall.

Ex. 104.

Thus it is said that the dominant minor thirteenth can be used in the major key if rising. The particular view taken is immaterial. The exposed octaves at (b) are allowable, because E♭ is merely a displacement of D.

6. The second inversion of the dominant thirteenth is not used, as the thirteenth against the fifth is extremely harsh. The last inversion is not used, as the thirteenth below the seventh is also harsh.

Ex. 105.

The fourth inversion is only used with the minor ninth. The major ninth should not be sounded below the third.

Ex. 106.

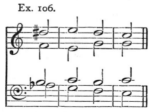

7. The following abbreviations will serve for these chords·
Dominant major thirteenth $V \frac{13}{7}$.

,,　　　minor　　　,,　　　$V^{♭}\frac{13}{7}$.

or $V \frac{7}{♯5}$.

8. The following examples of combined appoggiaturas or suspensions resolving into dominant harmony should be memorized. Alternative analyses are given.

Ex. 107.

(1) (*a*) dominant thirteenth with eleventh.

(*b*) double appoggiaturas or suspensions of fifth and third of dominant seventh.

(2) (*a*) dominant thirteenth with ninth.

(*b*) Upward and downward resolving suspensions or appoggiaturas of the third and fifth of dominant seventh.

(3) (*a*) Incomplete dominant thirteenth with ninth (a true dominant discord should contain the seventh).

(*b*) Appoggiaturas of the third and fifth of dominant seventh.

(4) As in (2).

9. As the resource discussed is merely a decoration of the dominant common chord and seventh, it will be obvious that the usual place for its employment will be either (*a*) at the start when it is necessary to establish the key, or (*b*) at the end of a sentence where a full close is desirable, or (*c*) at intermediate places where a new key has to be established (a new V to I with I or both V and I in inverted positions).

10. **Ear-tests.**

The above should also be transposed into the key of the tonic minor.

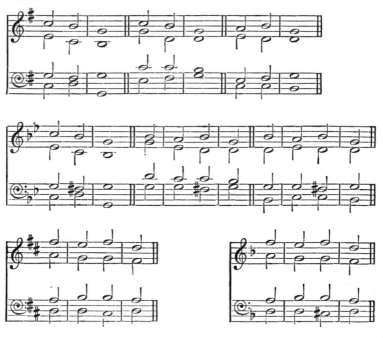

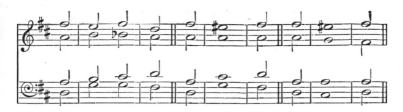

Use also examples in paragraph 8.

Exercises.

(1) Precede and follow the given chords by other appropriate harmonies; treat any discords higher than the seventh as suspensions or appoggiaturas.

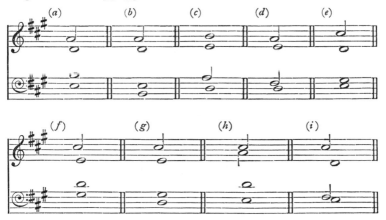

(2) Precede and follow the given chords by other appropriate harmonies; treat discords higher than the ninth as suspensions or appoggiaturas.

(3) Precede and follow the given chords by other appropriate harmonies, treating them as true chords of the thirteenth.

(4) Harmonize the following, introducing the resource discussed in this chapter (S. A. T. B.):

(5) Elaborate the following with the resource discussed in this chapter; alter anything except the bass; and figure the result:

(6) Fill in the harmony where omitted; figure the result:

(7) Harmonize the following basses for S. A. T. B., using the various resource discussed at the points indicated:

(8) Add in the blank spaces chords of the dominant seventh and ninth with appoggiatura of the third resolving:

(see Ex. 95.)

(see Ex. 95.)

(9) Add in the blank spaces chords of the dominant seventh with appoggiatura of the fifth resolving (see Ex. 96):

(10) Add in the blank spaces chords of the leading and

diminished seventh (with third from leading note displaced and resolved while the chord remains); see Ex. 98:

(11) Add true chords of the thirteenth in the blank spaces (see Ex. 99):

(12) Ditto with addition of minor ninth (see Ex. 100):

(13) Write original examples introducing the dominant seventh with sharpened fifth (major keys); see Ex. 103:

(14) Decorate the dominant chords as in Ex. 107:

CHAPTER IX

ADDITIONAL EXERCISES

1. It is advisable to have various types of problems in order to get familiar with the resource of harmony and the different demands made upon the capacity of the student. Further, it is a bad plan to adhere to one type of question.

2. I. **Figured Bass.** (*a*) This is the least useful type of question, as it settles the chord progressions. All therefore that the student can do is to attempt to write a melodious soprano part and correct inner parts. Care should be taken to vary the pitch of the soprano, so as to avoid dullness. The part should rise to at least one climax, and particular care should be taken to make the cadences satisfactory in their arrangement. The cadences at the end of the second and fourth phrases require the effect of finality. Therefore the root of the final chord of the Full Close should as a rule be in the top part. In other cases, where a note is common to the two chords, it should not be repeated in the melody. Exceptions will, of course, occur.

Ex. 108.

poor   good

Melodic tautology should be avoided.

Ex. 109.

bad   good

(*b*) Similarly, an inelegant part caused by the juxtaposition of two notes of the same name, one of them chromatically altered, may be avoided by a redistribution of the parts.

Ex. 110.

poor

(*c*) As it is an examiner's aim to find out a student's knowledge of chords, he will naturally include chords that require special treatment. In this connexion bear in mind:

(1) Cases in which the seventh in the dominant seventh may rise;

(2) The treatment of diminished and augmented triads in root position;

(3) The dominant major ninth must be sounded above the third unless resolving while the chord remains: it must be sounded above the third in the chord of the leading seventh;

(4) The thirteenth must be sounded above the seventh;

(5) Special treatment of some diatonic sevenths;

(6) The use of the melodic minor scale in harmonization.

(*d*) It is unfortunate that in the system of figuring a formula may mean one thing at one time, and another thing at another. But an examiner seizes on this to test the candidate's knowledge.

(1) 7 generally implies $\frac{7}{5}$. But when followed by a 6 on the same bass note it implies a suspension of the root of a chord.

Ex. 111.

6   7   6   7   6

(2) $\frac{4}{2}$ if resolving into a 6 on the note below means $\overset{6}{\underset{2}{4}}$.

When followed by a note below, with horizontal lines after the figures, it implies a suspension or appoggiatura. When the bass leaps from $\frac{4}{2}$ and does not resolve on the note below, $\frac{4}{2}$ implies two passing notes. $\overset{6}{\underset{2}{4}}$ in a similar case implies three passing notes.

Ex. 112.

(3) $\frac{6}{4}$ may imply the chord of the $\frac{6}{4}$ or two unessential notes, or the incomplete dominant thirteenth, or a retardation.

Ex. 113.

Such figuring as the following may trap the unwary :

Ex. 114.

(*e*) Sometimes the essential figuring only is given and students are required to put in their own unessential notes—passing and auxiliary notes, appoggiaturas, suspensions, &c. Care must be taken to obtain a fair distribution of them between the parts, and not to overload any single part with them.

Ex. 115.

If the bass give any indication of any figure, it is better to try to use it in the added parts.

Ex. 116.

But care must be taken to vary it and give it a rest, to prevent its degenerating into a tag.

(*f*) In all problems in music always look ahead. If the bass move up to a high note, the soprano should usually come down to meet it, or at any rate get into position so as to avoid overlapping.

Ex. 117.

(*g*) Whether the bass be figured or not, the student should see if it contains any sequential passages. If so, the soprano at any rate should also be sequential in conjunction with the bass.

Further, if the bass of two phrases starts or ends in a similar manner, it is intended that the soprano should likewise exhibit statement and response.

Ex. 118.

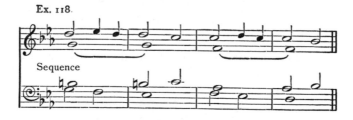

Beginning of first phrase :

Beginning of a later phrase :

Ending of one phrase :

Ending of another :

It is often quite good to introduce in the response some little variation from the original statement. But there is no harm in the exact reproduction of a section either in the same or a new key in the course of the problem.

3. II. **Unfigured Bass.** This leaves the choice of harmony to the student, and demands also the formation of a good melody. The various points to be remembered have already been discussed under other headings.

Two common faults should be specially noted :

(a) If the bass have a repeated or tied note weak to strong, the note on the strong accent must not be treated as a concord, but as a discord, if moving one step downwards.

Ex. 119.

(*b*) Beware of using a six-four on the strong accent, unless resolving into a $\frac{5}{3}$ or its equivalent.

Ex. 120.

4. III. **Harmonization of Melodies.** This tests the sense of harmonic progression, and the power of forming a good bass. The student should look up Chapter V. Many of the points mentioned there are applicable. Add :

(*a*) A repeated or tied note weak to strong should have the harmony changed on the strong beat. At a cadence this is vital.

Ex. 121.

(*b*) If the repeated note fall one degree, direct or ornamentally, it is usually a suspension.

Ex. 122.

(*c*) If a melody is sequential, aim at reproducing the sequence in the added parts.

Ex. 123.

(*d*) Be careful to lead up to the bass of the cadences, thus avoiding anticipating them.

5. IV. **Given inner part.** As this type of problem is more difficult, only the easiest exercises will be given. To this inner part the remaining three parts must be added. This tests at one and the same time the power to construct a good soprano and bass. The given part is the alto or tenor of a simple chord progression with the addition of a few unessential notes. The student should first of all settle the cadences and modulations, then add the bass, and finally the remaining parts. He must never allow himself to write dull harmony or a poor melody because of the uninteresting nature of the given middle part.

An example of the type of work is given in the Exercises.

6. V. **Writing a sentence introducing given chords or combinations.**

This type of question tests the knowledge of the treatment of various chords, and the ability to use them in a musical way.

(*a*) Note if any chords are specially suitable for cadences, and reserve them for these points. For example, the six-four on the dominant, or a suspension of the dominant chord over the tonic note.

Ex. 124.

(*b*) If any chords foreign to the tonic key are given, make the necessary modulations at the right places. If the chord of B flat were given in a problem commencing and ending in C major, the chord would occur in the key of F towards the end.

(*c*) Be careful to resolve all discords properly.

For an example, see pp. 95, 96.

7. VI. **Writing a sentence introducing prescribed modulations.**

Look up Chapters IV and V.

Aim at some imitation in the phrases.

If there are two phrases, it is well to attempt to make their openings correspond.

If there are four phrases, the second or fourth, or both, may imitate the first in their openings, and the fourth may imitate the cadence of the second. The third phrase usually subdivides into two smaller sections, and a corresponding portion of the first phrase may be imitated.

8. VII. **Ground Bass.** This is a bass repeated a few times but varied in treatment each time. At the present stage nothing but the most elementary treatment will be required.

Plan:

(1) State the bass alone.

(2) First repetition harmonized with plain chords and a few unessential notes.

(3) Second repetition harmonized with suspensions as characteristic feature.

(4) Third repetition harmonized with passing and auxiliary notes ; end with tonic chord.

In the first harmonization of the bass, establish the tonic ; in the second and third repetitions use appropriate modulation, first to the sharp side or relative key, and then to the flat side.

9. Examples.

Figured bass.

Ex. 125.

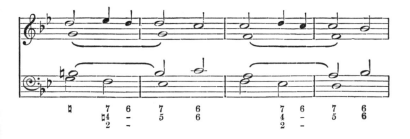

Unfigured bass.

Ex. 126.

Melody harmonized.
Ex. 127.

(a) It is common to avoid a Full Close in the tonic by following the dominant by the dominant of the relative minor.

Any of the three previous examples (Ex. 125, 126, and 127) could be the result of any one of the three types of question illustrated. Ex. 125 might have been an unfigured bass or a melody. Ex. 126 might have been a melody or figured bass. And Ex. 127 might have been a figured or unfigured bass.

10. Similarly, any of them might have resulted from the setting of the alto or tenor as the given part.

11. Again, Ex. 125 might have resulted from the following form of question: Begin as follows (bars 1–4 given) and modulate to D minor, C minor, B flat major, and back to G minor. The others could be re-stated in the same way.

12. Finally, they could all be the result of a question in this form: Write sixteen bars beginning and ending in the tonic key, introducing the following chords in any order appropriate, and making the necessary modulations. Ex. 127 would be the result of such a question, beginning and ending in F major, and introducing the following chords:

Ex. 128.

The chords may be introduced in any order, and in any time value, but with exact arrangement given.

It will thus be seen that all the above questions are merely tests in different aspects of the same thing. The result in each case must be a piece of intelligible music.

Ground Bass.

Ex. 129.

This working has been purposely made very simple and innocuous. It is sufficient at this elementary stage for the student to use his material correctly. Really musical students would probably produce something much more artistic. It is given as an example of what may be expected from the average student.

Exercises.

(1) Add parts for S. A. T. in accordance with the figures:

This period contains twelve bars.   There is no necessity to maintain a rigid pattern of sixteen bars.   In fact variety is desirable.

(2) Add parts for S. A. T. in accordance with the figures:

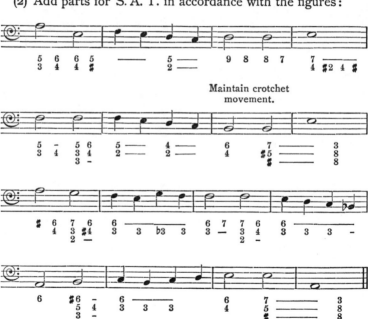

Maintain crotchet
movement.

(3) Add parts for S. A. T. to the following unfigured Basses:

(a)

(b)

(c) Maintain crotchet movement.

(1)

(1)

(1) When a tied bass note has been retained for the whole of the previous bar, the note on the succeeding strong accent need not be treated as a discord.

(d)

(4) Harmonize the following melodies for S. A. T. B. :

(1) Maintain crotchet movement.

(5) Add the remaining parts to the following, producing plain chord progressions with a few unessential notes:

(*a*)   Alto.   (See foot-note *.)

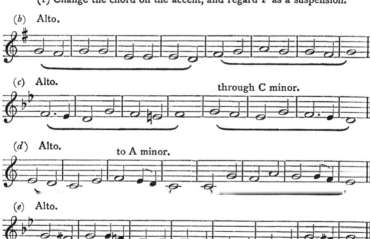

(1) Change the chord on the accent, and regard F as a suspension.

(*b*)   Alto.

(*c*)   Alto.   through C minor.

(*d*)   Alto.   to A minor.

(*e*)   Alto.

* Example of type of result required:
Tenor part given.

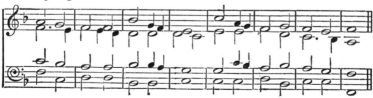

(*f*) Tenor.

(*g*) Tenor.

(*h*) Tenor.

(*i*) Tenor.

(*j*) Tenor.

(6) Write eight-bar sentences, divided into two phrases of four bars each, introducing the following chords :

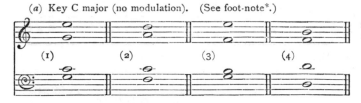

(*a*) Key C major (no modulation). (See foot-note*.)

(1)   (2)   (3)   (4)

* Example of type of result required. (Numbered chords given.)

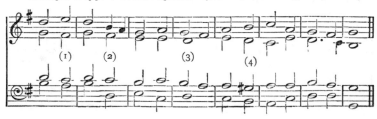

(1)   (2)   (3)   (4)

(*b*) Key G major (no modulation).

(*c*) Key F major (no modulation).

(*d*) Key D minor (no modulation).

(*e*) Key A major (with modulation).

(*f*) B♭ major (with modulation).

(*g*) Key **C** major (with modulation).

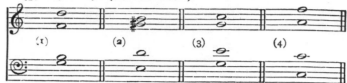

(7) Begin as follows, and in eight bars (two phrases):
  (*a*) Modulate to A minor and back to C.

  (*b*) Modulate to D minor and back to C (same start).
  (*c*) Modulate to F major and back to C (same start).
(8) Begin as follows, and in eight bars (two phrases):
  (*a*) Modulate to C major and back to A minor.

  (*b*) Modulate to F major and back to A minor (same start).
  (*c*) Modulate to E minor and back to A minor (same start).
(9) Begin as follows:

and proceed thus:

Bars 5–8, responsive phrase through B minor to Full Close in
        A major.
  „ 9–10, sub-phrase, modulation to G major.
  „ 11–12,   „   „   E minor.
  „ 13–16, back to D major.

(10) Begin as follows:

Bars 5–8, responsive phrase through F major to C major.
  „ 9–10, sub-phrase, modulation to B flat major.
  „ 11–12,   „   „   G minor.
  „ 13–16, back to D minor.

(11) Ground Basses (three repetitions in each case, in addition
to the statement):

(*e*)

(12) Add parts for S. A. T., introducing unessential notes:

(*a*)

(*b*)

(1) Let the upper parts move on the accents.

(*c*)

(2) Maintain crotchet movement over semibreves in some part, and imitate the bass of the succeeding bar. Crotchet movement should be fairly continuous throughout.